A
GUIDE
TO
NAVAJO
RUGS

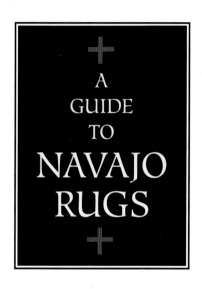

A
GUIDE
TO
NAVAJO
RUGS

WESTERN NATIONAL PARKS ASSOCIATION
Tucson, Arizona

ISBN 10: 1-877856-26-6
ISBN 13: 978-1-877856-26-6

Library of Congress Cataloging-in-Publication Number 92-62470

Written by Susan Lamb
Design by Christina Watkins
Photography by George H. H. Huey
Editorial by Ron Foreman

Printed in China by Imago
22 21 20 19 18   7 8 9 10 11

Published in the United States by Western National Parks Association
12880 N Vistoso Village Dr.
Tucson, AZ 85755

Western National Parks Association (WNPA) is a nonprofit education
partner of the National Park Service. WNPA supports parks across the
West, developing products, services, and programs that enhance the
visitor experience, understanding, and appreciation of national parks.
Learn more at www.wnpa.org.

For information or wholesale inquiries, please contact publishing@wnpa.org.

Western
    National Parks
    Association

CONTENTS

This booklet describes the basic characteristics of today's most common Navajo rug styles. But every rug, like its weaver, is an individual. In *Walk in Beauty,* Mary Kahlenberg and Tony Berlant describe Navajo textiles as manifesting their weavers' "place among people, their integration with the landscape, and their oneness with the spiritual forces of life."

In times past, weavers had few opportunities to talk about their work with anyone who lived more than a few miles away. As a result, distinct regional styles emerged because weavers only shared what they knew with their children and nearby neighbors.

In some cases, traders at local posts fostered particular designs based on popular notions of how a Navajo rug "should" look or on trends in home decorating. Traders also provided dyes and yarns that have influenced the colors and techniques weavers used in their rugs.

Many traditional weavers still depend entirely upon their own resources, however. They raise the sheep and shear, wash, card, and spin the wool themselves. They dye it as their mothers taught them, with native plants such as wild walnut, lichen, and rabbitbrush, or use the wool in its natural colors.

After stringing a home-made loom, a Navajo weaver sits on the ground and begins weaving at the bottom of the *warp*. As the weaver works, the completed part of the rug is rolled under to keep it out of the way, and the weaver must remember every nuance of the design until it is finished.

Navajo rug styles are still evolving. A "newstyle Crystal," for example, is very different from an "oldstyle Crystal." And today, a rug exhibiting a particular regional style may have been woven anywhere. Weavers also may depart from, combine, or overlap recognized "Navajo standard" styles. The guidelines in this booklet will pinpoint a rug's style about 95 percent of the time.

Four styles are recognized by their colors alone: Ganado, Klagetoh, Two Grey Hills, and Burntwater. The three styles of rugs that are woven in bands of color are distinguished by the designs within those bands: Chinle, Wide Ruins, and Crystal. Several other rugs are identified today by their designs: Eyedazzler, Teec Nos Pos, Storm, and Pictorial. Finally, the most recent, New Lands style, is woven in a particular design using only certain colors and an unusual weaving technique.

In buying a Navajo rug, consider whether it is neatly woven and symmetrical, with a nicely balanced overall design. But if you fall in love with a rug because something about its colors and design speaks to you, then that is the rug you should have.

———————

Italicized terms are explained in the Glossary, page 40.

✝

CHIEF

The Chief "blanket" is the earliest established weaving style known. The name comes from the high status of those Pueblo and Plains people to whom the Navajos (who do not have chiefs) traded them.

A Chief blanket today is distinguished by its square shape and by its plain design in blue and red, black and white. When the four corners of a Chief are folded to meet at the center, the design is the same as when it is unfolded.

The basic pattern has evolved over time, in four phases. The first Chiefs were woven in plain stripes of blue, white, black, and brown. Then *bayeta* became available, replacing brown. During this second phase, weavers also added short red bars to the design.

Third phase Chiefs are the most popular today. They are a little more elaborate, with stepped triangles in addition to the stripes of the original Chiefs. Rose-colored wool is sometimes used instead of red.

Finally, in the fourth phase, the stripes have been subsumed into squares against a solid background. Fourth phase Chiefs are rarely woven today.

"They say Spiderwoman did weave like that.
From her, everyone started weaving."
Roger Curley, Ganado, Arizona

First Phase Chief, #29122, 60 x 60 inches
Katherine Yazzie, Piñon, Arizona

Second Phase Chief, #29521, 47½ x 36 inches
Evelyn Curley, Ganado, Arizona

Third Phase Chief, #RL101, 57 x 51 inches
Nellie Smith, Klagetoh, Arizona

✦

GANADO

A Ganado rug always has a red background. For this reason, it is sometimes called a "Ganado Red." Typically, the black, white, and grey design is based on a central diamond or two. The edges of this central shape are embellished with geometric flourishes. *Serrates*, crosses, zigzags, and simple geometric shapes decorate the corner spaces outside the central design. A Ganado rug usually has a dark border.

Trader John Lorenzo Hubbell first popularized Ganado style rugs, promoting them by catalog to households in the eastern states. They are named for the little town of Ganado, where in 1878 Hubbell founded a trading post, which still operates today as Hubbell Trading Post National Historic Site. Ganado was named for a very important Navajo leader whom the Spanish called Ganado Mucho, or "Many Cattle."

Because of its long history and wide distribution, many people consider Ganado a "classic" Navajo rug style.

✦

"My grandmother make a real small carding board for me to card wool. It came out something like two inches. So I use it just to play with, and every time Grandmother was carding I would imitate her, trying to do what she was doing."
Marie Oskey, Ganado, Arizona

Ganado, #H.T.P.1990, 36 x 62 inches
Evelyn Curley, Ganado, Arizona

9

+

KLAGETOH

Klagetoh rugs resemble Ganados, but a typical Klagetoh is dominated by its grey background. The weaver uses black, white, and red in a design which is usually centered on an elongated diamond.

Except for the red, the different wools used are natural colors, although black wool may be enhanced with commercial dye. Sometimes, the grey will be brownish or even distinctly tan, depending upon the fleece.

Although the distinctions between Ganado, Klagetoh, Two Grey Hills, and Burntwater are made strictly on the basis of color, the first two styles tend to have simpler designs than the other two.

The name comes from a small settlement south of Ganado, and means "Hidden Springs."

+

"Shear the wool then card the wool. Card a lot of wool for the warp, depending on the size. Spin the wool several times to make it thin...And if you are going to make red wool you have to build a fire and boil it and spin it. It takes many days just to do that."
Mary Lee Begay, Chinle, Arizona

Klagetoh, #H911, 38 x 59 inches
Mae Benally, Klagetoh, Arizona

TWO GREY HILLS

True Two Grey Hills rugs are woven of natural, undyed, handspun wool in designs of white, black, and brown. Weavers produce subtle shades of these basic hues by carding together wool from different sheep. The wool is often quite fine, requiring more weaving time but resulting in an exquisite rug. Because of the considerable time and effort required to prepare handspun wool, rugs made from it may cost twice as much as those of comparable size made from commercial yarns.

The design does not represent hills. Two Grey Hills rugs are named for a village in New Mexico. They tend to have a plain, dark border, but the patterns are often more complicated than those of a Ganado or a Klagetoh. Like other styles with borders, many Two Grey Hills rugs have a *spirit line*.

"I put the spirit line in every time I weave.
You weave a line going out and in again.
Your design is your thinking, so you don't border
that up. It's your home and all that you have.
And so if you close that up, you close everything
up—even your thinking and your work."
Mae Jim, Woodsprings, Arizona

12

Two Grey Hills, #MH502, 31 x 43 inches
Maralin John, Two Grey Hills, New Mexico

13

✢ BURNTWATER

A rich combination of earth tones and pastels distinguishes Burntwater rugs. Warm colors such as brown, sienna, mustard, and rust are accented with a sparing use of pale, milky colors including rose, green, blue, white, and lilac.

This newer style, an elaboration of traditional Two Grey Hills designs, is usually woven in the *vegetal colors* favored by weavers of the Wide Ruins/Burntwater area south of Ganado. With these additional design elements—geometric spirals, head-to-head triangles, stepped diagonals, multiple borders—some weavers may use twenty or more colors in large Burntwaters.

✢

"It [the spindle] doesn't go backwards, it goes toward you. Your mind and prayers are connected to it. Medicine men have ceremonial doings for it, in the Hozhooji (Blessingway)."
Mae Jim, Woodsprings, Arizona

Burntwater, #29517, 24 x 36 inches
Brenda Spencer, Wide Ruins, Arizona

15

CHINLE

The Chinle is one of three styles of banded rugs, which usually have no borders. Chinles are the simplest of the banded rugs, with stripes of plain color alternating with bands containing repeated geometric designs such as *squash blossoms*, stacked chevrons, and diamonds. They may have *railroad tracks*, as well.

Chinle rugs tend to be pastel or restrained colors, with lots of natural greys, whites, golds, and greens. However, they may also be bright and bold—in black, white, and red, for example.

This style, though named for the town of Chinle, is now woven everywhere in the Navajo Nation. It is one of the most commonly woven rugs because the design is relatively straightforward and can take less time to weave than more elaborate designs.

"Making a rug is not just anything. You have to be careful. Even the tools you work with; you must take good care of them. You don't kick them and break them up. You keep them for your children's children to use them."
Evelyn Curley, Ganado, Arizona

Chinle, #K-3, 23 x 37 inches
Irene Harvey, Ganado, Arizona

17

WIDE RUINS

Wide Ruins is the most elaborate banded rug style. It also has broad stripes of plain color and some stripes with geometric designs, but weavers add very narrow bands with delicate motifs plus thin, straight lines of contrasting colors. Shapes within the broader bands are often outlined with a different color. Wide Ruins are usually the most finely woven banded rugs.

Wide Ruins colors tend to be deep, somber vegetals—browns, olives, maroons, and mustards—accented sparingly with an elemental color such as white, red, or black.

The Wide Ruins style evolved from the Chinle. Occasionally, a weaving falls between the two styles, and is considered either a complicated Chinle or a simple Wide Ruins, depending upon its colors and on the weaver's origins.

"When I start to weave there will be a spider. And my mother say: 'Don't bother it. Let it run around on your loom. [Otherwise] you might run out of wool. And it make the rug worth a lot more,' she say."
Vannie Mann, Spider Rock, Arizona

Wide Ruins, #28954, 29 x 40 inches
Betty R. Roan, Wide Ruins, Arizona

19

✝

CRYSTAL

The Crystal style of banded rugs features a very specific difference: the "wavy" line, produced by alternating two or three different colors of *weft* strands.

Crystal rugs typically group three bands of wavy lines or a solid color between one or two complex bands. Generally, the complex bands are patterned with *squash blossoms*, but they may feature other motifs such as arrows, stars, crosses, triangles, bearpaws, or diamonds.

The colors used in weaving Crystals tend to be muted earthen colors such as rust, grey, and rich brown. Sometimes, pastel greens, pinks, or yellows are also used.

These banded rugs are the "new" style of Crystal, which has developed in the area around the Crystal Trading Post in western New Mexico since the 1930s. Previously, a Crystal-style rug was a bordered rug with a central design woven of natural colors, perhaps with a touch of red.

"My aunt! I was small and she would tell me: learn. She would make me and chase me over there to do it. In one summer I learned! Now I am glad that she used to chase me to the loom ..."
Mary J. Barker, Wide Ruins, Arizona

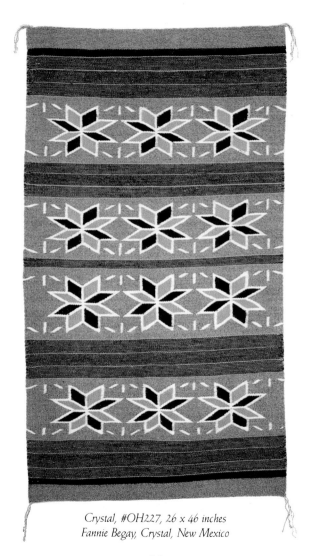

Crystal, #OH227, 26 x 46 inches
Fannie Begay, Crystal, New Mexico

21

✝
EYEDAZZLER

Eyedazzler rugs are just that: busy, eyedazzling weavings of any combination of colors. Usually, the design is a simple geometric shape—chevron, diamond, *serrate*, triangle—repeated through the entire rug. There may be a border. Occasionally, the eyedazzler design will appear only in blocks set off against a solid background.

Eyedazzler is one of the earliest styles of rugs, and was influenced by serape blankets worn in New Mexico. They came into their own in the 1870s, when traders imported bright *Germantown* wool. Weavers suddenly had a brilliant new range of colors to work with, so this design emphasizes the effects of combining contrasting hues. Within ten years, the *aniline* dye used to produce Germantown yarns was directly available to Navajo weavers.

"In our tradition, you are not supposed to finish a rug at night. I asked my Mom: 'why?' And she said: 'Just leave a little to where you can see the string. Then all you have to do is put it together in the morning. Then I said, 'No, I want it off tonight, so I can clean it and all that.' She said: 'You'll go blind.'"
Laura Moore, Nazlini, Arizona

Eyedazzler, #D140, 30 x 39 inches
Pauline Nez, Klagetoh, Arizona

23

✝

TEEC NOS POS

Always surrounded by a wide border and filled with an exuberant variety of motifs, Teec Nos Pos (Tēs-Nōs-Pōs) rugs are often large. Because of their size and complexity, Teec Nos Pos weavings can be very expensive.

An elaborate center is often enhanced with stylized feathers and arrows. Clawlike, angular hooks extend from the points of diamonds and triangles; zigzags are everywhere. The wide borders of a Teec Nos Pos often contain a *lightning path*.

Contrasting colors outline many elements, and there are lots of diagonal lines. There is no rule for colors in a Teec Nos Pos rug, although of course they must harmonize.

Teec Nos Pos is a bold, busy, exciting design. Many experts believe it developed from pictures of Persian rugs; others see no connection. The name comes from a settlement in the northeast corner of Navajo country. It means "Cottonwoods in a Circle." However, similar rugs are woven from Mexican Water on the west to Beklabito, New Mexico, on the east.

"I do it out of pride because my grandmother did and my mother did. I want to do it to carry on tradition…I guess it's pride and tradition."
Lenora Davis, Ganado, Arizona

Teec Nos Pos, #K-3, 34 x 41 inches
Bessie Lorgo, Teec Nos Pos, Arizona

STORM

The Storm rug style is distinguished by its design, not colors. This abstract design is supposed to contain the Navajo symbolism for a storm, but it is widely believed that a trader in Tuba City developed and promoted it among local weavers, perhaps after hearing a Navajo legend, or possibly from a printed flour sack. It is the only rug style that purports to be an abstract portrayal of a natural event.

In the middle of the rug is a rectangle, representing the center of the universe. Four rectangles in the corners of the rug stand for the homes of the four winds or, by some interpretations, the four sacred mountains of the Navajo world. Zigzag "lightning" connects these with the center.

Storm rugs usually have a dark border that is often embellished on one side with geometric "teeth." The space between the main design and the border usually contains stylized elements, such as clouds and water beetles. Arrows, feathers, and geometric designs abound.

"They used to pass out the papers and say: 'you weave one like this.' ...Grandmother that passed away, she never did copy one. She didn't want the paper. She used to say: 'I'll weave my own pattern'."
Mikes Daughter Frank, Jedito, Arizona

Storm, #29512, 30 x 46 inches
Sarah Tsinnie, Tuba City, Arizona

27

✠

PICTORIAL

A Pictorial rug portrays a bit of Navajo reality; a woven journal of the features of a weaver's daily life.

Many Pictorials are landscapes with a *hogan*, a corral and pickup truck, a woman in a long skirt. Sheep, cattle, and horses are often shown, too. The landscape usually includes rock formations, trees, ponds, and clouds. Railroad trains, panel trucks emblazoned with soft drink logos, and even aircraft also show up in pictorials.

Pictorial rugs are woven in colors appropriate to the subject matter—blue skies, green junipers, black or white sheep. Borders, if any, are usually dark.

Many Pictorials are still woven without perspective or shading, but some weavers are producing surprisingly realistic pictures, considering the medium.

Occasionally, a weaver will make a replica of a flag, or weave a motto such as "Home Sweet Home." Though technically Pictorials, these are usually referred to as "specialty rugs."

"Sometime I usually weave all day and herd sheep and help around the house and chopping wood…It seem like every time you look up there is a jet plane."
Eli Van Winkle, Nazlini, Arizona

Pictorial, #MH406, 36 x 42 inches
Louise Nez, Cedar Ridge, Arizona

SANDPAINTING

These pictorial rugs are based on ceremonial *sandpaintings*, and thus are considered somewhat controversial. They portray the spiritual realm of the Navajo people. Depending upon the ceremony for which the original sandpainting was made, these extraordinary weavings may show supernatural beings and their magical implements, the spirits of the earth and sky, and powerful creatures and plants. Common elements in sandpaintings include snakes, feathers, lizards, and *whirling logs*.

Sandpainting rugs are square. Their colors have a definite significance. Certain hues represent the cardinal directions. Rainbows are red, white, and blue. The background is usually tan, like plain sand.

The area around Shiprock, New Mexico, is known for Sandpainting rugs. A medicine man named Hosteen Klah, who used real sandpaintings in curing ceremonies, is believed to have been one of the first people to weave them.

"'Pray to it and talk to it,' that is what my mother says to me...I hear her praying in the morning to her loom."
Mary J. Barker, Wide Ruins, Arizona

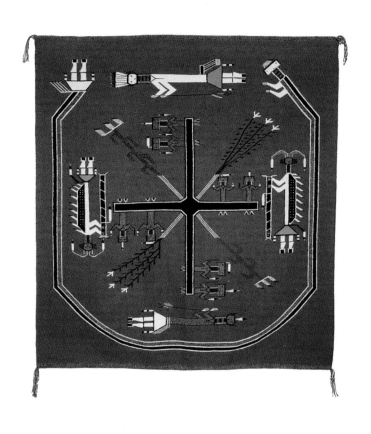

Sandpainting, 60 x 60 inches
(weaver unknown)

31

YEI

Yei (or *ye'ii*, pronouned "yay") rugs depict yeis, the supernatural "Holy People" who communicate between the Navajo and their gods. They are shown face-front as tall, slender, stylized figures carrying rattles, pine boughs, or yucca strips. Usually, the long body of the "rainbow yei" surrounds them. This design has elements of some sandpaintings, but it is not used in ceremonies. It is controversial, also. Some weavers of Yeis have a ceremony performed to show respect and to keep harmony in their lives.

In color, anything goes in the weaving of a Yei rug. A dozen or more hues may be used.

These intriguing rugs are strongly representative of the Navajo culture. Navajo ceremonialism centers on a desire for healing: not only physical health, but also mental, emotional, spiritual, and even material well-being. The "Holy People" portrayed in Yei rugs are believed to restore health when called upon in a properly conducted ceremony.

"They have to have a sing done by a medicine man. That's how they weave them."
Helen Kirk, Kinlichee, Arizona

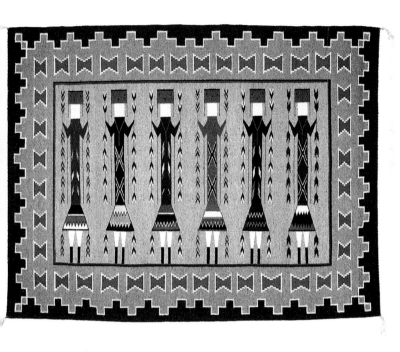

Yei, #29544, 51 x 67 inches
Minnie Coan, Red Rock, New Mexico

33

YEIBICHAI

Yeibichai (yay-ba-chay) rugs depict ceremonies in which human dancers impersonate yeis. There are usually six dancers, often in profile and with one leg bent as if dancing. Sometimes the six dancers, who are men, alternate with six women. Other figures may include a lead dancer, a following clown known as a "water sprinkler," the medicine man, and the patient for whom the ceremony was performed. All of these are rendered as realistically proportioned human beings.

Weavers use lifelike colors in Yeibichai rugs. Although it is a nighttime ceremony, it is seldom shown as a night scene.

Occasionally, ceremonies other than the Yeibichai are shown. A few weavers depict "Squawdances" (the Enemyway) or "Firedances." The area around Many Farms, in the center of the Navajo Nation, is known for Yeibichai rugs.

"They say that you are not supposed to say that [your rug is ugly.] The rug can hear you and so don't talk about it that way in front of it."
Mary J. Barker, Wide Ruins, Arizona

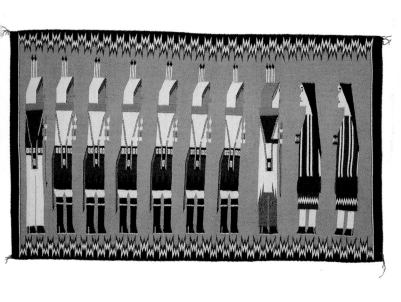

Yeibichai, #K-3, 30 x 51 inches
Elouise Bia, Ganado, Arizona

35

TREE OF LIFE

The Tree of Life design portrays a tree or cornstalk growing from a basket. Occasionally a different plant, such as a thistle, will be represented. There may also be several branched trees or stalks of corn shown.

Birds of many brilliant colors perch on and around the Tree of Life. Sometimes, other familiar creatures—butterflies, rabbits, or squirrels—are also present.

The background is usually a pale color, to set off the bright, *aniline* hues used to weave the birds. Some of the birds are recognizable species such as cardinals, jays, or woodpeckers. They may be flying, perched, or even on the "ground" around the basket at the bottom. Bright flowers and vines are often shown, too. Generally, Tree of Life rugs have a dark, plain border.

The Cedar Ridge area is known for fine Tree of Life rugs.

"I was born under a tree. A long time ago, it used to be like that. You were just born under a tree."
Ellen Smith, Wide Ruins, Arizona

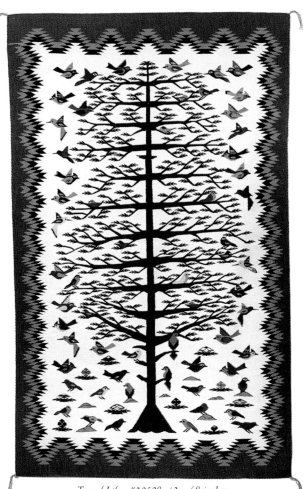

Tree of Life, #29508, 42 x 68 inches
Rena Mountain, Cedar Ridge, Arizona

NEW LANDS

The New Lands style is the most recent development in Navajo weaving. New Lands rugs combine Burntwater colors with a Teec Nos Pos design, and enhance the effect with a *raised outline*.

Trader Bruce Burnham initiated this new style from his trading post in Sanders, Arizona. He recruited local experts in vegetal dyes to produce a myriad of lovely colors and encouraged local weavers to use them, even grouping together harmonious colors in "kits" for their use.

These rugs are woven in spectacular, complicated designs and a rainbow of natural hues. Like Teec Nos Pos rugs, they tend to be large weavings, and can be quite expensive.

The name comes from the area around Sanders, called the New Lands because many residents were relocated there from traditional homelands.

"I usually talk to the people I sell my rug to; make sure it's going to a good home and they're going to take care of it. I guess it's like a baby—you put all that work into it, take care of its problems—you want someone who's going to appreciate it."
Lenora Davis, Ganado, Arizona

New Lands, #29373, 36 x 58 inches
Susie Begay, Sanders, Arizona

39

GLOSSARY

Aniline: Inexpensive, easy-to-use dyes derived from coal tar, often used to produce bright colors.

Bayeta: From baize, a red woolen cloth imported by the Spanish and unravelled by Navajo weavers to make yarn. The deep red color came from cochineal, a dye made from crushed insects.

Germantown: A yarn named for the town in Pennsylvania where much of it was manufactured.

Hogan: A traditional one-room Navajo home of earth and wood.

Lightning Path: A series of elongated X or H shapes around a border, sometimes alternating with squash blossoms.

Railroad Track: Contrasting colors alternated to produce a very narrow, checkered stripe.

Raised Outline: A technique in which diagonal lines are emphasized by the use of additional weft strands.

Sandpainting: A picture used in a Navajo ceremony; composed of thin trails of sand, pollen, charcoal, or ground minerals and plants. It is destroyed during the ceremony.

Serrate: A stairstepped diamond pattern (from the Spanish for "notched").

Sing: A lengthy ceremony composed of as many as five hundred songs performed by a medicine man during several days or nights to restore a person's inward harmony and health.

Spirit Line: A line of contrasting color of wool extending from the background to the outer edge of the rug.

Squash Blossom: A design made up of triangles, which resembles a stylized, angular flower.

Vegetal Colors: Wool colors obtained from natural plant dyes. Some collectors have begun to use this term to describe the colors of a rug made of commercially-dyed yarn when the colors are similar to those derived from plants.

Warp: The strong, lengthwise threads on a loom into which colored wool is woven.

Weft: The colored, crosswise threads that are woven into the upright, or warp threads, to produce a design.

Whirling Logs: Also known by the German term "swastika," a four-armed motif found among diverse peoples of the world. In Navajo, it conveys a sense of holiness. It can represent the cardinal directions, or the movement of spirits between worlds.

"I don't like to just sit here.
I only like it when I am weaving."
Ellen Smith, Wide Ruins, Arizona

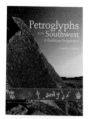

Petroglyphs of the Southwest:
A Puebloan Perspective
By Conroy Chino
ISBN 978-1-58369-140-3

A Guide to Zuni Fetishes
By Susan Lamb
ISBN 978-1-58369-028-4

A Guide to Hopi Katsina Carvings
By Rose Houk
ISBN 978-1-58369-038-3

A Guide to Indian Jewelry
of the Southwest
By Georgiana Kennedy Simpson
ISBN 978-1-58369-000-0

A Guide to Pueblo Pottery
By Susan Lamb
ISBN 978-1-877856-62-4

A Guide to American Indian Folk Art
By Susan Lamb
ISBN 978-1-58369-065-9

A Guide to American Indian Bead Work
By Rose Houk
ISBN 978-1-58369-109-0